Simple Acts, Matter Of Fact

50 River Beneath 50 Ocean

Make A Difference
Vol. 1

CHANDAN MALANA

Chandan Malana Publication House

ISBN: 9798851251627

Cover design by:
Chandan Malana

Published by
Chandan Malana
Publication House

Preface

In a world often consumed by chaos and uncertainty, it is easy to underestimate the power of simple acts. We find ourselves entangled in the complexities of daily life, overlooking the profound impact that even the smallest gestures can have on the lives of others. However, in "Simple Acts, Matter of Fact," author Chandan Malana invites us to explore the profound potential within these seemingly ordinary deeds.

This remarkable collection of poems and quotes serves as a poignant reminder that each one of us possesses the ability to make a difference in the world. Through his eloquent words, Malana unveils the transformative power of compassion, kindness, and empathy. He gracefully weaves together vivid imagery, evocative metaphors, and heartfelt emotions to create a tapestry that celebrates the beauty of human connection.

"Simple Acts, Matter of Fact" is a journey that takes us through the various facets of our existence, encouraging us to reflect on our actions and the impact they have on those around us. Malana explores themes of love, resilience, forgiveness, and social responsibility, shedding light on the untapped potential within our hearts and souls.

The pages of this book are filled with wisdom that transcends boundaries and resonates with readers from all walks of life. Each poem and quote acts as a gentle nudge, a gentle reminder that our lives are interconnected, and that our choices and actions can ripple outwards, touching the lives of others in ways we may never fully comprehend.

Whether it is the uplifting verses that inspire us to persevere through challenges, the tender words that stir our compassion, or the profound insights that provoke us to question our roles as individuals in society, "Simple Acts, Matter of Fact" encourages us to embrace our humanity and embrace the power of simple acts to create lasting change.

As you delve into the verses and quotes within these pages, may you find solace, inspiration, and renewed hope. May you be reminded that every smile, every kind word, and every act of compassion has the potential to ignite a spark within the hearts of those around you. By embracing the simplicity of these acts, we can collectively reshape the world, one gesture at a time.

Chandan Malana's "Simple Acts, Matter of Fact" is a testament to the profound impact we can have on the world when we choose to engage with compassion, authenticity, and a genuine desire to make a difference. It is an invitation to embark on a journey of self-reflection and discovery, reminding us that within each of us lies the power to create a more compassionate and interconnected world.

So, let us venture forth, armed with the knowledge that simple acts matter, and with the conviction that we can, indeed, make a difference.

Message From Author

B.Sc Bioinformatics
M.Sc Microbiology
PG.Diploma In Aroma Technology

Dear Readers,

I am Chandan Malana, the author of the book "Simple Acts, Matter Of Fact". This book has 50 Creating a Difference poetic masterpieces and 50 Making a Difference quotes. It is the

First volume of the series
"Make A Difference".

Writing poetry has been my
hobby since my school days,
and it has grown into a
passionate pastime. I am very
proud and excited to finally
share my work with you.

If you enjoy this book, I would
love to publish a second
volume. Please feel free to
contact me at any time with
your feedback, comments,
and suggestions.

Thank you for your support!

Best regards,

Chandan Malana

Simple Acts, Matter Of Fact

50 River Beneath 50 Ocean

Make A Difference

Vol. 1

CHANDAN MALANA

Chandan Malana Publication House

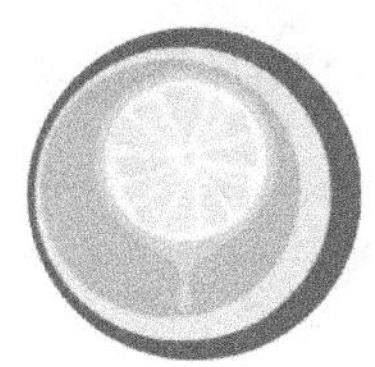

Contents

Activism Is My Rent

Activism is the fire that ignites my
soul,

A duty I embrace to make this world
whole.

It's my rent for living, a purpose I
pursue,

To leave a lasting impact, to make a
difference, too.

In the face of injustice, I take a stand,

Raising my voice for those without a
hand.

With every step I take, with every
word I say,

I strive to create change, to light a
brighter way.

Activism is my melody, my powerful
song,

Uniting hearts and minds, where we
all belong.

With empathy as my guide,
compassion as my force,

I seek to build bridges, to shape a better
course.

Inequality and prejudice, they cannot
prevail,

For I am fueled by justice, a wind that
will sail.

I march on the streets, I rally with the
crowd,

Advocating for rights, proclaiming
them aloud.

Activism is a seed I sow in fertile
ground,

Nurturing hope, where despair may be
found.

I cultivate understanding, I sow seeds
of peace,

Fighting for a world where injustice
finds release.

I challenge the norms, I break down
walls,

For in unity and equality, humanity
recalls,

That each life matters, no matter how
small,

And through activism, we rise and
stand tall.

Together we can shape a world of
harmony,

Where love and acceptance are the
currency.

Activism is the bond that unites us all,

Empowering voices, breaking down
every wall.

So let us rise together, in this shared
quest,

To make a difference, to give it our
best.

Activism is our duty, a debt we must
repay,

For living on this planet, let us make
our way.

Chandan Malana

Quote 1

"With every breath that I take, I feel the need to push for a change, Activism is my rent for living, And I pay it every day with giving. I pay my rent with activism, It's my contribution to the planet's prism, Standing for what's right and fair, Making my voice heard everywhere."

Chandan Malana

Be The Change, One Person To Rearrange

In a world where darkness may persist,

One person's light can truly assist.

With strength and passion, they embark,

To make a difference, leave their mark.

For in their heart, a fire burns bright,

A beacon of hope, a guiding light.

They strive to lift the oppressed and
weak,

To inspire change, the bold and meek.

Through acts of kindness, both big and
small,

They heed the silent, the unheard call.

They lend a hand, they offer their care,

Spreading love and compassion
everywhere.

Their words, like poetry, weave a tale,

Igniting hearts, making them prevail.

They challenge norms, they break the
mold,

Encouraging others, making them bold.

They plant the seeds of love and trust,

Nurturing dreams, they never combust.

With empathy, they mend the broken,

Transforming lives with words
unspoken.

With each step taken, they pave the
way,

To brighter futures, a new array.

They shatter barriers, they bridge
divides,

Uniting souls with love that abides.

No task too great, no challenge too
tough,

Their spirit unwavering, they've had
enough.

For they believe in the power of one,

To change the world, until it is done.

So let us all rise, embrace the call,

To stand for justice, and never fall.

For one person can make a difference,
it's true,

And everyone should try, starting with
me and you.

Chandan Malana

Quote 2

"One person's choices and deeds, Can sow seeds for the greater needs, With courage and determination in eye, Everyone should try, to make a difference amplify."

Chandan Malana

Believe To Achieve

In a world of vast dimensions,

Where dreams meet limitations,

There stands a truth, profound and clear,

One person's actions can reverberate near.

No need for fame or fortune's touch,

Nor titles grand or influence much,

With heart ablaze and a soul so bold,

You hold the power to break the mold.

For in the depths of humble hearts,

Lies the strength to heal and restart,

A simple act, a helping hand,

Can bring light to darkness, across the land.

Believe in yourself, embrace the might,

To challenge wrongs, bring justice's
light,

With steadfast faith, you'll surely find,

The power within to leave no soul
behind.

From a kind word to a selfless deed,

You sow the seeds of hope and need,

Each small action, like a gentle rain,

Nourishes the world with love's sweet
refrain.

In a sea of doubt and despair,

Your compassion, a beacon rare,

It ripples outward, far and wide,

A force of change, a rising tide.

For greatness lies not in wealth or
fame,

But in the hearts that refuse to tame,

Their burning desire to make things
right,

To illuminate the darkest night.

So heed this truth, let it be your guide,

One person's difference can't be denied,

With faith as your compass, stand tall
and strong,

For you, dear soul, have the power to
belong.

Chandan Malana

Quote 3

"No matter the size of the action you take, Faith in one's power can never be fake, Don't wait for grandeur or fame to commence, One person's impact can make a difference."

Chandan Malana

Beyond The Dollar

In a world where wealth is sought with might,

Many strive to fill their pockets tight.

But true worth lies beyond monetary gain,

In the power to make a difference, we ascertain.

To make a buck, a fleeting endeavor,

Yet making a difference lasts forever.

It takes courage, compassion, and a
noble heart,

To uplift others, playing a
transformative part.

A dollar earned may bring temporary
cheer,

But changing lives brings a purpose
clear.

The impact we leave on hearts and
minds,

Defines our legacy for future times.

A difference made resonates far and
wide,

Touching souls, bringing hope like a
gentle tide.

It's not about accumulating wealth and
fame,

But the lives we touch, leaving an
everlasting flame.

In every action, great or small,

We possess the power to stand tall.

With kindness, love, and empathy's
embrace,

We shape a world where compassion
takes place.

While wealth may come and quickly
fade,

Making a difference does not evade.

It demands commitment, dedication
true,

To change the lives of those we never
knew.

So let us strive for a purpose profound,

To make a difference, let our actions
resound.

For in this noble quest, we find our
true worth,

Creating a legacy that transcends the
earthly berth.

It's easy to make a buck, that's plain to
see,

But making a difference sets our
spirits free.

With open hearts and hands reaching
out,

We'll leave a lasting impact without a
doubt.

Chandan Malana

Quote 4

"Anyone can earn a dollar bill, But to create change takes real skill. It requires more than just making money, An effort to transform lives, oh how sunny! Making money is simple, a formula quite clear, But making an impact that matters, that's a true career. For it takes more than wealth to leave a lasting impression, A contribution to the world, a conscious expression."

Chandan Malana

Breaking The Chains Embracing Change

I stand with strength, I break the chains,

No longer bound by life's constraints.

I refuse to surrender to fate's decree,

For I am the force that shapes my destiny.

No more will I bow to the whims of
time,

I'll rise above, against the paradigm.

With courage as my shield, I boldly
strive,

To make a difference and truly come
alive.

The things that once held me back, I
defy,

With unwavering spirit, I reach for the
sky.

I embrace the challenge, the unknown,

To transform the world into a better
home.

In the face of injustice, I take my stand,

A beacon of change, extending a helping hand.

With empathy and kindness, my weapons of choice,

I'll fight for justice with an unwavering voice.

No longer accepting the status quo,

I'll confront the shadows that linger and grow.

Through perseverance and grit, I'll blaze the trail,

And inspire others to rise and prevail.

Inequality and hatred, I cannot accept,

With love and unity, their walls I'll intercept.

I'll sow seeds of compassion, nurture them strong,

For in unity's harmony, we all belong.

The world may tremble, doubters may sneer,

But my resolve remains steadfast and clear.

I'll forge a path where dreams become real,

Where every heart knows its worth and zeal.

So join me now, let's ignite the flame,

Together we'll rise, nevermore the
same.

For I am the change, the hope that will
persist,

I am the difference, in a world that
can't resist.

Chandan Malana

Quote 5

"I'm done with inaction, I've made up my mind, It's time to take action and not be left behind, The things I cannot change, I'll put to rest, But the things I can't accept, I'll change for the best."

Chandan Malana

Care And Compassion: A Society's Greatest Passion

In a society harmonious and bright,

Where compassion reigns and hearts take flight,

Those with means and strength, so bold,

Embrace the duty, a story to unfold.

For in this realm of togetherness,

A symphony of empathy, no less,

The fortunate souls with hearts
aflame,

Yearn to uplift, make a difference, and
tame.

Hand in hand, we strive to thrive,

For in unity, our souls revive,

With open arms and tender care,

We nurture dreams, banish despair.

With steadfast love, we bridge the
divide,

Spreading hope, compassion as our
guide,

No walls or boundaries can restrain,

The spirit of kindness that shall
remain.

For the weak and weary who seek
respite,

A shelter of solace, a comforting light,

We offer support, a soothing embrace,

A haven of warmth, a saving grace.

In this tapestry of life we weave,

Each thread of kindness, a gift we
leave,

A legacy of compassion, unfurled,

A testament to how we change the
world.

So let us remember, with hearts
aligned,

To reach out and care, the way
designed,

For when we nurture, with love
entwined,

A brighter future, we all shall find.

In a society that shines so bright,

We'll walk together, through day and night,

For the beauty lies in the bonds we share,

When we take care of one another, we truly dare.

Chandan Malana

Quote 6

"For a society where we thrive, Together we must help others to survive, Our purpose being to lend a hand, And support those who can't stand."

Chandan Malana

Catching, Throwing: Life's Going

I've learned a truth, a lesson so profound,

In life's great game, I've come to astound,

To catch and hold, with mitts both secure,

Leads to a life that's empty, unsure.

For in our hands, lies the power to
share,

To make a difference, to show we care,

The catchers' mitt, it traps and
confines,

But throwing back, that's where the
magic shines.

With open palms, we embrace the
world's call,

To lend a hand, to rise above the small,

No longer passive, no longer confined,

We step forth boldly, with hearts
aligned.

A single act, a gesture so profound,

Can change a life, turn darkness around,

Through empathy's touch, we ignite a spark,

And bring hope to those lost in the dark.

For kindness ripples, in waves it will flow,

From one to another, a continuous glow,

Each throw we make, creates a ripple's trace,

Spreading love and joy, in every embrace.

So let us be givers, with open hearts,

Not just receivers, playing our parts,

The catchers' mitts, we'll lay them
aside,

And let compassion and love be our
guide.

In every moment, we hold this chance,

To make a difference, to take a stance,

With gratitude, we'll embrace life's
track,

Throwing back goodness, never holding
back.

So remember this wisdom, embrace it
true,

With open hands, you'll find what you
pursue,

For life's not just catching, it's about
the throw,

To make a difference, let kindness
grow.

Chandan Malana

Quote 7

"Life's a give and take, it's not just for you to make, Don't just catch it all, let something go in your wake, Be ready to throw something back, with all your might, Balance the scales of life, embrace the give-and-take light."

Chandan Malana

Chance For Change, Seek The Range

I have one life, a precious gift,
bestowed upon my soul,

A chance to leave a mark, a purpose, to
play my destined role.

My faith, a guiding light, demands that
I embrace,

To strive, to serve, to make a
difference, in every time and place.

Wherever I may wander, wherever my
feet may tread,

I'll lend a helping hand, uplift those
filled with dread.

For in this vast expanse, I see hearts
longing for change,

And with every act of kindness, a
ripple I'll arrange.

Whenever the sun rises, painting the
skies so grand,

I'll seize the fleeting moments, with
courage firmly in my hand.

No moment too small, no task too
humble or weak,

With passion, I'll pursue my purpose,
the difference I'll seek.

For as long as I'm blessed, with breath
in my very core,

I'll journey on with fervor, leaving
footprints on the shore.

Time may be finite, but impact
transcends the years,

A legacy of love and kindness, erasing
sorrowful tears.

With whatever I have, be it wealth or
simple means,

I'll use them as my tools, to mend
fractured human beings.

For riches lie not in possessions, but in
hearts that intertwine,

And in unity, we'll forge a world where
compassion truly shines.

To try, to strive, to alter destinies
unknown,

To wipe away despair, with empathy
firmly sewn.

In every moment's grace, an
opportunity to embrace,

The power to make a difference, in this
vast human race.

So let us join together, hand in hand,
side by side,

In unity we'll conquer, the odds we
shall defy.

For when our spirits align, a symphony
we'll create,

Harmonizing change, as we uplift and
elevate.

*I have one life, one chance, to make a
difference profound,*

*To leave a lasting legacy, with love and
kindness crowned.*

*And when my time has come, and my
journey's at its end,*

*May the world be better for it, with
hope that I did send.*

Chandan Malana

Quote 8

"One life, one chance, let's make it right, To make a change, a noble fight, Anytime, anywhere, let's lend a hand, For a better world, let's take a stand."

Chandan Malana

Change Takes Time, Patience Is Prime

Don't expect change with morning's
light,

For transformation takes its flight.

Though unseen, its power grows,

In depths of hearts, its presence shows.

With every step, a small advance,

Creating ripples, a subtle dance.

In every word, a seed is sown,

That sprouts and spreads, unknown,
but known.

In silence, whispers fill the air,

A quiet force, beyond compare.

The choices made, the paths we take,

Can mold a world, make no mistake.

The tiniest actions, like drops of rain,

Merge to form rivers, break the chain.

The impact builds, like waves that rise,

Transforming lives before our eyes.

So don't lose hope when progress seems
slow,

For change's roots continue to grow.

Each act of kindness, no matter how
small,

Can make a difference, change it all.

Like stars that shine in darkest night,

Change illuminates, brings forth light.

It's in the moments, both big and small,

That transformation touches all.

Embrace the journey, with patient
heart,

Knowing change's power can never
depart.

Though it may not happen overnight,

Its influence shines, a guiding light.

So have faith in the impact you make,

Even if progress feels hard to take.

For change is constant, a force unseen,

Making a difference, fulfilling a dream.

Chandan Malana

Quote 9

"Be patient, dear friend, change takes time, Though not always visible, it's truly prime, The impact it makes, we may not see, But rest assured, it's happening, it's meant to be."

Chandan Malana

Change The World With One Small Step

In a world so vast, with dreams untold,

Resides a power within each soul.

With hearts ablaze, a fire ignites,

To make a difference, with shining lights.

With every step, we forge our way,

Guided by purpose, come what may.

With hands outstretched, we lend a
hand,

To heal the wounds in this troubled
land.

Through words of kindness, we can
inspire,

Igniting hope, to lift spirits higher.

A simple act, a gesture so small,

Can spark a change, break down every
wall.

In unity we find, a strength profound,

United hearts, a harmonious sound.

For when we stand as one, side by side,

Our impact grows, far and wide.

No task too great, no mountain too
high,

With determination, we'll reach the
sky.

With love as our compass, we'll
navigate,

Transforming lives, erasing hate.

From the depths of despair, we'll bring
light,

Illuminate darkness, banish the night.

Through compassion's embrace, we'll
mend,

A world in need, we'll fiercely defend.

So let us rise, with hearts full of zeal,

In every action, let kindness reveal.

For in our hands, lies the power to
bestow,

A legacy of love, as we bloom and grow.

Each of us holds the key, to make a change,

With commitment and will, we rearrange.

Together we'll shape a future bright,

Each making a difference, with all our might.

Chandan Malana

Quote 10

"Let's take the first step and make the vow, To spread kindness and love from here and now, With commitment and passion to do our part, Together we can change the world's beating heart."

Chandan Malana

Create Waves, One Stone Brave

I alone can't change the world, it's true,

But I hold a stone, with a purpose
anew.

In my hand, a chance to make a
difference,

To cast it across waters, with resolute
insistence.

This stone, a catalyst, small but
profound,

Creates ripples, echoing far beyond the
ground.

With each gentle splash, a message is
sent,

Touching lives, inspiring hearts, where
it's meant.

In schools, I'll teach, igniting young
minds,

Planting seeds of knowledge, where
wisdom finds.

I'll nurture their dreams, guiding them
with care,

For in their success, I'll find joy to
share.

In communities, I'll lend a helping
hand,

Supporting the needy, taking a stand.

Through service and compassion, I'll
extend,

A beacon of hope, to those who depend.

With words as my weapon, I'll write
and speak,

Addressing injustices, the strong and
the weak.

I'll raise my voice, for the silenced ones,

Empowering their stories, till justice
runs.

In nature's embrace, I'll sow seeds of
green,

Protecting the Earth, a duty
unforeseen.

By tending to forests, and cleansing the
air,

I'll preserve the planet, with devoted
care.

Through acts of kindness, I'll spread
love's embrace,

Embracing diversity, erasing all trace,

Of prejudice and hatred, that divide
our land,

Uniting humanity, with an
outstretched hand.

Though one stone may seem small in
the tide,

Its ripples can't be denied, far and
wide.

I may not change the world on my own,

But together, we'll make a difference
known.

Chandan Malana

Quote 11

"One stone cast, a ripple effect, Many hearts touched, a chain connect, A single act, a force for good, A greater impact, than we understood."

Chandan Malana

Difference You Make, Every Step You Take

In the realm of life's vast expanse,

Resides a truth, a precious chance.

What you do, with each passing day,

Shapes the world in a unique way.

Like ripples in a tranquil lake,

Your actions cause effects to wake.

Embrace the power that lies within,

For it's your choices that truly win.

Do you seek to heal the wounded soul,

To offer kindness, make others whole?

Or will your path be one of strife,

Leaving scars, dividing life?

The difference made, it's yours to
choose,

A symphony of notes, you can't refuse.

Will you sow seeds of love and grace,

Or sow discord and leave a bitter
trace?

With open heart and gentle touch,

You have the power to uplift much.

Bring laughter to a weary face,

Spread hope, and leave a lasting trace.

In every word, in every deed,

Consider well the impact you'll lead.

For even small acts, with purpose true,

Can inspire greatness, both old and
new.

Let empathy guide your every stride,

In unity, let compassion abide.

For in this tapestry of existence,

Your mark can make a world of
difference.

So choose with care, embrace your role,

Let kindness be the anthem of your
soul.

For what you do, with love or disdain,

Will echo on, and forever remain.

Chandan Malana

Quote 12

"Every action you take, every step you make, Creates a new path, a difference to stake, So choose with care, the direction to go, A difference to make, that will continue to grow."

Chandan Malana

Embrace The Fire
Of Your Desire

Be who you're meant to be, let your
light shine,

Embrace your purpose with a heart so
fine.

For deep within you, a flame does
reside,

Ignite it boldly, let it be your guide.

In a world that yearns for hope and
desire,

You hold the power to set it on fire.

With passion as your fuel and love as
your spark,

Make a difference, illuminate the dark.

God's design for you is uniquely spun,

A masterpiece, woven when time
begun.

Embrace your talents, let them bloom
and grow,

And watch the world flourish, bask in
your glow.

Don't hide your essence, let it radiate,

In every action, let kindness dictate.

With empathy and grace, touch lives
around,

Create ripples of change, profound and
profound.

Each soul has a purpose, a path to
tread,

With every step forward, fears may be
shed.

Believe in yourself, for you hold the
key,

To unlock the greatness that longs to be
free.

Embrace your uniqueness, stand tall
and strong,

Embody virtues that inspire and
belong.

For when you're true to yourself, my
dear friend,

You'll inspire others to rise and
transcend.

The world awaits your gifts, so share
them wide,

Spread love and compassion, let it
collide.

With hearts aflame, together we'll
aspire,

To make a difference and set the world
on fire.

So be who God meant you to be, my
dear,

With purpose and passion, have no
fear.

For in your journey, you'll find your
own way,

And set the world ablaze, making
miracles each day.

Chandan Malana

Quote 13

"When we embrace our truest self, We unlock a power beyond wealth, For we were made to shine and inspire, And set the world on fire with our desire."

Chandan Malana

Help The Ones Around You

In a world consumed by numbers, vast and grand,

Let not your heart be swayed by their demanding hand.

For true worth lies not in the tally of souls,

But in the difference made, as compassion unfolds.

So fret not over figures, whether high
or low,

Instead, focus on the one whose spirits
may be low.

Extend a helping hand, let kindness be
your creed,

For in lifting just one, you sow a noble
seed.

Begin with the person nearest, close at
hand,

For their burden might weigh heavy,
hard to withstand.

A smile, a listening ear, a gentle touch,

Can bring solace and comfort, oh, how
much!

For change starts with a single act of
care,

A ripple that spreads, a burden we can
share.

Never underestimate the power within,

To ignite a spark, kindle hope, and
kinship begin.

The world may seem vast, with
challenges untold,

But remember, it's through individuals
we mold.

Each life you touch, a chance to make a
difference,

To inspire, to uplift, with heartfelt
persistence.

Let love guide your actions, let
empathy prevail,

For in the smallest deeds, the grandest
tales unveil.

A compassionate heart, a beacon in the
night,

Shining light on darkness, turning
wrongs to right.

No matter the numbers, no matter how
vast,

The impact of kindness will forever
last.

For in helping one person, you create a
chain,

A legacy of compassion, healing hearts'
pain.

So cast aside worries of numbers and
strife,

Embrace the calling to transform one
life.

For in this noble quest, a truth is clear:

Helping just one person can change the
world, my dear.

Chandan Malana

Quote 14

"Focus not on amount, but the heart's gift you can mount, Sow seeds of change, starting small with one in range, Pour love into one person's cup, bringing hope and lifting them up, For one life touched and made better, is a ripple effect that lasts forever."

Chandan Malana

Heroes Sharing Responsibility In Life

In a world where shared responsibility
thrives,

Where it's easy to turn away and hide,

Some souls emerge, shining oh so
bright,

Heroes who make a difference, day and
night.

They see the struggles, the challenges
we face,

Refusing to let apathy take its place,

For they understand the power they
possess,

To heal, to uplift, to bring success.

Not their child, nor their community,

Yet they embrace the call for unity,

They step forward, their hearts filled
with grace,

Guiding us toward a better, kinder
space.

When others say, "It's not my world,
not my concern,"

These heroes step up, eager to learn,

They grasp the weight of each problem
and pain,

Seeking solutions, not letting it wane.

Through acts of kindness, they ignite a
spark,

Inspiring others to make their mark,

They lend a hand, they offer their time,

Building bridges, forging a sublime
rhyme.

For in a tapestry of lives intertwined,

We realize our destinies are aligned,

By sharing responsibility, we grow,

Together, the seeds of change we sow.

So let us honor those who see the need,

The heroes who plant the altruistic
seed,

They teach us all to rise and to aspire,

To make a difference, to fan the fire.

In this world where shared responsibility gleams,

Let's join hands, unite in our dreams,

For when we stand together, side by side,

We become heroes, changing the tides.

Chandan Malana

Quote 15

"When faced with problems oh so great, It's easy to ignore and say "no way," But heroes see what's at stake, And take on the challenges day by day."

Chandan Malana

Hope Alone Won't Suffice

In a world where shadows play,

We can't just hope for a brighter day.

With hearts entwined, we must take a stand,

And work together, hand in hand.

Love, obscured by hurt and fear,

Yearns to rise, crystal-clear.

It's up to us to break the chain,

Unleash compassion's healing rain.

Through toil and sweat, we'll find the
way,

To make a difference, come what may.

No longer bound by apathy's snare,

We'll spread kindness, showing we
care.

For family, our hearts will strive,

Keeping love's flame alive.

With open arms and tender grace,

We'll build a haven, a sacred space.

Friends, like stars, will guide our path,

In unity, we'll conquer wrath.

Together we'll rise, above the strife,

Transforming darkness, igniting life.

Our neighbors, near and far away,

We'll embrace, without delay.

In each connection, a chance to find,

The beauty that unites mankind.

So let us toil, let us reclaim,

Love's essence from shadows' claim.

With every action, every word we
speak,

A brighter day is what we'll seek.

No longer bound by fear's tight grip,

Love's tender touch, we'll let it slip,

Into the hearts of all we meet,

Creating a world that's truly sweet.

Chandan Malana

Quote 16

"To hope for a brighter day is not enough, We must work hard to make love rise above, Push through the hurt and fear that block the way, And dig it out, let love lead the play."

Chandan Malana

Hopeless Is Not A Creed

No one has a right to sit and despair,

For there's a world in need, calling us to care.

In every corner, troubles unfold,

Yet within our hearts, the power to uphold.

No one has a right to simply retreat,

When hope's flame flickers, in need of
our heat.

Let us rise from doubt, embrace the
fight,

With hands joined together, we'll make
things right.

No one has a right to be passive, you
see,

For the winds of change blow,
beckoning thee.

In each small action, a chance to make
amends,

To mend broken souls, and to make a
difference.

No one has a right to let dreams fade,

When aspirations linger, eager to be
played.

With determination as our guiding
star,

We'll shape tomorrow, no matter how
far.

No one has a right to surrender the
quest,

When injustice persists, we must
protest.

With voices united, echoing strong,

We'll challenge the odds, till justice
belongs.

No one has a right to sit in despair,

When kindness and love are the
burdens we bear.

In every act of compassion, we ignite,

A spark of hope that can pierce through
the night.

No one has a right to shun their part,

For within our souls, lies the power to
start.

With open hearts and minds, we'll take
a stand,

To build a brighter future, hand in
hand.

No one has a right to sit and feel low,

For our purpose is clear, it's time to let it show.

In every step we take, the world we'll rearrange,

And make a difference, through hope's endless range.

Chandan Malana

Quote 17

"It's easy to feel lost in despair, To surrender to hopelessness, unfair, But there's work to do, a mission to pursue, No time to waste, let's see it through. With determination, your strength will renew."

Chandan Malana

I Have But One Life To Live

I have one life, a precious gift to hold,

A single chance, a story to unfold.

In this vast world, I strive to find my way,

To make a difference, each and every day.

With purpose burning bright within
my soul,

I'll leave my mark, achieve a noble goal.

For life's true measure lies not in mere
wealth,

But in the impact I leave in good
health.

Through words and deeds, I'll spread
kindness wide,

A beacon of hope, a constant guide.

In every smile, a ray of light I'll share,

To uplift hearts burdened with despair.

In giving love and lending helping
hands,

I'll bridge the gaps, unite divided lands.

For unity's strength lies in diversity,

Together we'll shape a world of unity.

With empathy, I'll see beyond the veil,

Embrace the hurting, their wounds I'll
gently heal.

In understanding, differences we'll
embrace,

And foster harmony, a sacred space.

Through knowledge gained, I'll strive
to educate,

Empowering minds, dispelling
ignorance's fate.

For education's key unlocks each door,

Enabling dreams to soar, forevermore.

With passion blazing like a fiery sun,

I'll fight injustice, till it's overcome.

For equality and justice must prevail,

As every voice deserves a fair, just sail.

So as I tread this path, I'll stand tall
and strong,

Knowing I have one life, where I
belong.

I'll make it count, leave footprints in
the sand,

A legacy of love, a difference made,
grand.

Chandan Malana

Quote 18

"I have but one life to live, one chance to make my mark, So every day I make a choice, to light a fire or let it grow dark, With each step forward, I leave a trail of purpose and meaning, Hoping to inspire others and keep their own dreams gleaming."

Chandan Malana

In Our Hands, A Better World to Expand

We hold the power, within our grasp,

To transform the world, our noble task.

With hearts ablaze, a vision so clear,

Together we'll rise, conquering fear.

In unity, we'll spread our wings wide,

Each step forward, with purpose as our
guide.

With empathy as our steadfast creed,

We'll sow compassion's transformative
seed.

Hand in hand, we'll mend what is
broken,

Words of kindness, the seeds we've
spoken.

In every action, big or small,

A ripple of change, inspiring all.

With open hearts, we'll bridge the divide,

From prejudice and hatred, we'll turn the tide.

Embracing diversity, celebrating the same,

We'll erase the boundaries, erase the blame.

Through education, we'll light the way,

Empowering minds, no darkness can sway.

Unlocking the potential, in every soul,

A brighter future, our ultimate goal.

We'll heal the wounds of our fragile
Earth,

Preserving its beauty, realizing its
worth.

Respecting nature, in every choice we
make,

Sustaining life, for future's sake.

In our hands lies the power to heal,

To lift each other, to truly feel.

A single act of love can ignite,

A chain reaction, reaching infinite
height.

So let us rise, united and strong,

With hope in our hearts, we'll right
every wrong.

Together we'll make a difference
profound,

A world transformed, where love is
renowned.

Chandan Malana

Quote 19

"With power in our hands held tight, We can make the world shine bright, A better place, just in our sight, Let's make a difference with all our might."

Chandan Malana

Inspiring Acts, Making a Difference with Facts

Regardless of whatever I do,

My purpose stands strong and true.

To make a difference, bright and clear,

In people's lives, both far and near.

With every word that I may say,

I strive to guide and light the way.

To touch a heart, to heal a soul,

And help them reach their ultimate
goal.

Through actions, big and small,

I'll be there to catch them if they fall.

To lend a hand, to ease their pain,

And let them know they're not in vain.

*In smiles exchanged and tears
embraced,*

A difference made, cannot be erased.

To bring hope where darkness thrives,

*And remind them of the love that
survives.*

*Through laughter shared and dreams
pursued,*

A difference made, forever imbued.

To inspire courage, ignite a spark,

*And lead them from shadows, out of
the dark.*

In kindness shown and empathy
shared,

A difference made, by those who cared.

To uplift spirits, mend broken hearts,

And rebuild lives, in all their diverse
parts.

Through passion unleashed and talents
revealed,

A difference made, a destiny sealed.

To empower others to find their voice,

And let their impact make a joyful
noise.

Regardless of whatever I do,

My purpose remains steadfast and true.

To make a difference, both big and small,

For in the end, it's the greatest gift of all.

Chandan Malana

Quote 20

"To make a difference in people's lives, A purpose that guides us, inspires and thrives, With each act of kindness, each word of care, We leave behind a legacy that lasts beyond compare."

Chandan Malana

It's Not What You Keep, But What You Give

In life's grand tapestry, we weave our
fate,

With actions that define our earthly
state.

Yet when we depart, and bid this world
adieu,

What remains of our deeds, both old
and new?

For what we do for ourselves, in self-serving glee,

Shall perish with us, like waves in a sea.

But when we extend our hearts to make a difference,

Our impact resonates with eternal persistence.

A selfless act, a helping hand extended,

Creates ripples of kindness that never end.

Through simple gestures, we shape a legacy,

Touching souls with love and empathy.

A smile shared, a burden eased,

Can ignite a flame that will never
cease.

For when we lift others from sorrow's
deep abyss,

Their spirits soar, forever finding bliss.

The seeds we sow in others' barren
fields,

Blossom into hope, as destiny reveals.

A kind word spoken, a listening ear,

Gives solace to hearts burdened by
fear.

When we lend our strength to those
who falter,

We ignite a spark, an unyielding alter.

And though we may depart this
transient plane,

Our goodness lives on, an eternal
refrain.

In the annals of time, our name may
fade,

But the echoes of compassion never
evade.

For what we do for others, beyond our
own strife,

Becomes a symphony, a melody for life.

So let us strive to leave a lasting mark,

To brighten the world, even in the dark.

For what we do for ourselves dies with
our breath,

But what we do for others conquers
even death.

Chandan Malana

Quote 21

"It's not what we take with us when we go, But how we touch lives and let kindness flow, For what we do for ourselves is temporary in scope, But the impact we make for others becomes an everlasting hope."

Chandan Malana

Join The Fight, Doing What Is Right

In a world filled with strife and despair,

A call to action, a plea in the air.

Fight for the things that ignite your soul,

But let your approach make a difference, make it whole.

With passion ablaze, let your voice
resound,

In melodies of change, let your words
be found.

Rhyme with conviction, each verse a
decree,

That sparks a fire in others to join the
journey.

When battling injustice, let kindness
be your shield,

For empathy and compassion are the
weapons we wield.

Seek common ground, bridge the
divide,

In unity, true power resides.

Be the beacon of hope, lighting the way,

Illuminate minds, let prejudice sway.

For true understanding, we must
strive,

To create a world where all can thrive.

Let your actions inspire, let them
ignite,

A *flame* in the hearts of those in the
fight.

For change starts small, but can grow
so vast,

When united, we overcome the
obstacles amassed.

Choose words that resonate, that touch
the heart,

Plant seeds of transformation, a
brand-new start.

In every stanza, let justice prevail,

And let your poetry be the wind in
justice's sail.

Be a catalyst for progress, a force to be
reckoned,

For in unity, the power lies, unbroken.

Lead by example, show others the way,

And make a difference, with each
passing day.

So *fight for the things that you deeply care,*

In rhymes and verses, let others be aware.

But do it in a way that will inspire, not divide,

And together, let's change the world, side by side.

Chandan Malana

Quote 22

"Fight for what you believe, but not alone, Do it in a way to make your passion known, And maybe, just maybe, others will see, And join with you, in this great worthy plea."

Chandan Malana

Justice And Peace: Let Love's Definition Lead

In a world of chaos, strife, and fear,

Where division reigns and love's unclear,

Imagine a place where hearts unite,

A paradise of peace, bathed in light.

If global citizens shared one view,

A common love that's strong and true,

Bound by compassion, understanding deep,

Harmony and justice, our souls shall keep.

No borders or boundaries, just pure grace,

Love's definition we all embrace,

Guiding our thoughts with kindness and care,

A difference we'd make, a world so fair.

No more hatred's venom, venom's sting,

Only compassion's melody would sing,

Hands reaching out, bridging every
divide,

With love as our guide, we'd surely
stride.

No more wars waged in the name of
greed,

Justice prevailing, fulfilling our need,

Equality and fairness for all to see,

United as one, we'd set our world free.

With love's definition etched in our
hearts,

Empathy and acceptance playing their
parts,

No more discrimination, no more
disdain,

In this paradise, love would forever
reign.

We'd heal the wounds, mend broken
trust,

Respecting each other, in love we'd
adjust,

The power of love, a beacon so bright,

Guiding our actions, leading us to
what's right.

So let's strive for a world of love's
embrace,

Where peace and justice leave no
empty space,

As global citizens, let's make the
change,

With a shared definition, our world
rearrange.

Chandan Malana

Quote 23

*"If we all embraced love as our guide,
And let kindness and compassion
coincide, Then peace and justice would
brightly shine, And the world would be
a paradise that's divine."*

Chandan Malana

Justice Demands A Price

Human progress, a path not guaranteed,

Nor automatic, nor easily conceived.

Justice's goal demands sacrifice, profound,

The struggle endured, as truth is renowned.

Every step taken, a price to be paid,

Suffering endured, as foundations laid.

With tireless exertions, we forge ahead,

Passionate concern, where hope is
spread.

Dedicated souls, with hearts strong
and true,

They make a difference, for me and for
you.

Injustice confronted, they bravely
fight,

Guiding us toward a brighter, fairer
light.

Their voices rise high, breaking
oppression's chains,

Through trials endured, their strength
sustains.

Their tireless efforts, a beacon so
bright,

Igniting a flame, to stand up and fight.

For progress requires more than mere
desire,

It demands action, fueled by a fire.

Through valleys of darkness, they
boldly tread,

For justice and equity, souls
widespread.

In each sacrifice made, a purpose
unfolds,

As their fervor ignites, the story
unfolds.

The struggle endured, with
unwavering might,

Their passionate hearts, a guiding
light.

Through hardship and toil, they pave
the way,

Their resolute spirit, it shall not sway.

For progress lies not in destiny's hand,

But in the tireless efforts of women
and man.

So let us join hands, united we stand,

For justice and progress, hand in hand.

With sacrifice, suffering, and struggle
endured,

We'll make a difference, our purpose
assured.

Chandan Malana

Quote 24

"In the journey for progress, we must understand, It's not automatic, nor in destiny's hand. Each step towards justice demands sacrifice and pain, But dedicated individuals make a difference, not in vain."

Chandan Malana

Let Our Hands Be The Catalyst For Change

In this vast tapestry of life's design,

No single soul can solely redefine.

For change, a symphony of voices weaves,

In harmony, the world's true colors cleaves.

A single candle, flickering with might,

Illuminates the darkest depths of night.

Yet, with the union of a thousand
flames,

A beacon bold, the world forever tames.

No mountain scaled or valley left
unturned,

Is conquered by a soul alone,
concerned.

Together, hand in hand, we shape the
course,

And breathe new life where hope had
shown remorse.

Each act, however small, can plant a
seed,

That blossoms into change with
gracious speed.

A word of kindness, tender and sincere,

Can heal the wounds that burden
hearts with fear.

For even drops of rain, when they
combine,

Become a mighty river, so divine.

No one can underestimate the power,

Of unity in every shining hour.

The brushstrokes of a painter, paint a
scene,

But it's the world's embrace that makes
it keen.

The poet's pen, its ink on parchment
spills,

Yet readers' minds, its message truly
thrills.

No hero stands alone in valor's might,

For all are part of change's radiant
light.

In unity, our voices blend and soar,

Creating ripples that will forevermore.

So let us join our hands, ignite the
flame,

And let our actions echo loud,
proclaim:

No one changes the world alone, 'tis
true,

And no one, standing still, can make a
difference, too.

Chandan Malana

Quote 25

"Each step we take, we are not alone, With every effort, a seed of change is sown, Together we rise, with hope and might, Changing the world with a unified sight."

Chandan Malana

Lifting Each Other

When you lift up another's spirit,

In that moment, you truly merit,

For as you share words of hope and
light,

You kindle flames that burn so bright.

Through your encouragement, hearts
ignite,

Dispelling shadows, bringing delight.

A commitment made to uplift and
inspire,

A beacon of hope, a soul's desire.

In the tapestry of life, a thread you
weave,

Through gentle words, you help others
believe.

With every act of kindness that you
show,

A difference is made, seeds of strength
you sow.

For when you encourage with love and
grace,

You touch a soul, leaving a lasting
trace.

A ripple effect begins to unfold,

Spreading positivity, breaking the
mold.

In the act of encouragement, a bond is
formed,

A lifeline extended, through storms, a
platform.

You become the wind beneath their
wings,

Empowering them to rise and sing.

With each word spoken, you ignite a
fire,

Fanning dreams and desires higher
and higher.

You offer support, a gentle embrace,

Guiding others to find their own space.

Encouragement is a gift, a treasure
rare,

It shows you truly care, beyond
compare.

For in lifting others, you find your own
way,

A heart filled with joy, come what may.

So, let us be encouragers, strong and true,

Making a difference in all that we do.

For when we uplift and inspire with persistence,

We create a world filled with hope and brilliance.

Chandan Malana

Quote 26

"Lift others up, and you will rise, As you make a commitment, cultivating ties, Encouragement given, a difference made, In their life, your light has stayed."

Chandan Malana

Light Up Life: Contributions That Lift Up Strife

In a world consumed by selfish pursuits,

Where individual desires take root,

Let us rise above the ego's sway,

And make a difference, come what may.

Reach out your hand to those in need,

With empathy and kindness, plant a
seed,

For it's in selflessness that true growth
lies,

And the power to change lives, in our
ties.

Let not ambition blind our sight,

To the struggles of others, day and
night,

For a single act of compassion, so
small,

Can make a difference and break down
walls.

Find a cause that stirs your heart,

A purpose that sets your soul apart,

For the world needs heroes, big and
small,

To stand up, to rise, and heed the call.

In a sea of voices, be the voice,

That champions justice, and makes the
choice,

To fight for equality, peace, and love,

A difference made, like wings of a dove.

Extend your love beyond your own,

To the forgotten, the silenced, the
unknown,

For in unity, strength will arise,

And the world will witness our shared
reprise.

Let compassion guide every deed,

In thought, in word, and every creed,

For in selflessness, we find our worth,

And make a difference, here on Earth.

So let us rise, united and strong,

And strive to right the world's wrong,

Make a difference, in every way,

For tomorrow awaits a brighter day.

Chandan Malana

Quote 27

"Let's shift our focus outward, towards the world we're living in, And seek to change what's wrong, instead of just giving in. For true fulfillment comes not from what we can gain, But from the impact we have on others, and how we ease their pain."

Chandan Malana

Making A Difference

In a world so vast and ever-changing,

A truth we often find, rearranging,

That in our quest to chase success,

It's the impact we make that truly
impress.

For when we lend a helping hand,

A ripple forms, across the land,

The power to touch a soul's despair,

And show them that someone does
care.

In giving love, without condition,

We find a purpose, a heartfelt mission,

For it's in selflessness we truly see,

The beauty of our own humanity.

A simple smile, a listening ear,

Can wipe away a lingering tear,

A kind word spoken, a gentle touch,

Can heal the wounds that hurt so much.

For in the act of making a difference,

We unlock within ourselves a resilience,

A strength that comes from deep within,

Igniting a fire that never dims.

To lift others up, to ease their strife,

Brings meaning and joy to our own
life,

For the impact we have on another's
heart,

Is where true fulfillment finds its start.

So let us strive to make our mark,

In this world, sometimes so stark,

To spread compassion, love, and cheer,

Knowing it's in giving that we
persevere.

*You may find that making a difference,
it's true,*

*Is the greatest gift you can ever
pursue,*

*For as you touch lives, both old and
new,*

*You'll find that making a difference
also makes you.*

Chandan Malana

Quote 28

"By making a difference for others we find, A sense of purpose that energizes the mind, Like a ripple effect, our actions inspire, Our own hearts and souls set on fire."

Chandan Malana

Making A Mark, Leaving A Spark

In life's vast stage, where moments unfold,

A truth profound, its wisdom behold,

If your presence lacks impact, my friend,

Your absence won't bring a noticeable end.

Like a whisper lost amidst the breeze,

Unheard, unnoticed, you blend with
ease,

Yet if you strive to leave an indelible
trace,

Your absence shall leave an empty
space.

For when your presence resonates and
shines,

Touching hearts, inspiring like vibrant
vines,

The void you'd leave would echo loud
and clear,

Your absence would pierce, causing
hearts to tear.

So seek to make a difference each
passing day,

Embrace the power you hold in every
way,

For even the smallest acts of love and
care,

Can ripple through lives, creating a
lasting flare.

When your presence radiates warmth
and light,

Illuminating paths with hope and
might,

Your absence, my dear, would lack the
same,

The world would yearn for your
presence's flame.

Each word you speak, each deed you do,

Has the potential to touch hearts anew,

But if you choose to remain in
shadows' dance,

Your absence won't spark a second
glance.

So let your presence be a force,
unyielding,

An essence that's felt, forever
appealing,

And when the time comes for you to
part,

Your absence shall linger, a poignant
art.

Remember, my friend, the power you possess,

To make a difference, to bring happiness,

For if your presence doesn't make an impact,

Your absence won't make a difference, in fact.

Chandan Malana

Quote 29

"Leave your mark, make an impact,
Your presence felt, a meaningful pact,
For if you're gone, and left no trace,
Your absence fades, with no lasting
grace."

Chandan Malana

Meal For One Is Where To Start

If you cannot feed a hundred people,
feed one,

In the shadows of hunger, let your
kindness shine like the sun.

For even the smallest act of
compassion, oh, how it can transcend,

A single soul nourished, a life on which
you can depend.

In this world of vast need, where
despair often prevails,

Be the beacon of hope, where humanity
unveils.

For it's not about numbers, but the
impact you create,

With love as your weapon, the
difference you can make.

Extend your hand to the hungry, to the
ones left behind,

Let your heart be their refuge, a
sanctuary they find.

For in the face of adversity, your light
can guide the way,

Transforming lives, bringing joy, with
each meal you lay.

For every morsel you offer, every plate
you provide,

The hunger pangs subside, and dignity
is amplified.

Remember, it's not just food you offer
on this blessed day,

But a glimpse of a future where
despair gives way.

See the gratitude in their eyes, as they
savor every bite,

The nourishment of body and soul, a
moment so bright.

For in that fleeting moment, as they
taste your care,

Their burdens grow lighter, their
hearts lifted in prayer.

The ripple of your kindness spreads far
and wide,

Inspiring others to join, to walk by
your side.

For if we all unite, each doing what we
can,

Together we can eradicate hunger, a
noble plan.

So, if you cannot feed a hundred
people, worry not,

Feed one, for it's in those small acts,
our true power is brought.

For with compassion as our guide, and
love as our source,

We can change the world, make a
difference, of course.

For in the tapestry of life, we are all threads intertwined,

Connected by a shared purpose, a hope we can find.

So, let us feed the hungry, one by one, till none remain,

And create a world where no soul hungers in vain.

Chandan Malana

Quote 30

"If a hundred hunger, and resources are scarce, Feed just one, for compassion knows no bounds to spare. For in the act of giving, we receive, A sense of purpose, of hope, of peace, And forging one's own fate and believe, That one small act can make love increase."

Chandan Malana

Moment's Chance, A Tapestry In a Trance

How wonderful it is, this truth so
clear,

That no moment's lost, no time to fear.

For each soul holds the power, strong
and bright,

To make a difference, bring change to
the night.

With hearts filled with love and minds
of grace,

We can weave compassion into every
space.

No need to wait, no need for delay,

Let's start today, and light up the way.

In every act of kindness, a ripple is
born,

Touching lives, leaving traces of hope
adorn.

From a simple smile to a helping hand,

Together we can create a world so
grand.

Let's bridge the gaps, break down the
walls,

Lift each other up when darkness falls.

Through unity and empathy, we shall
succeed,

In building a world where all can be
freed.

A single word of encouragement and
care,

Can bring solace to hearts burdened by
despair.

No task too small, no gesture too slight,

In our hands lies the power to ignite.

Let's embrace diversity, embrace the
unknown,

For in our differences, true strength is
sown.

No longer bound by prejudice and hate,

We can weave a tapestry of love, a
beautiful fate.

So let us rise, let our voices resound,

In harmony, let our intentions be
found.

For in our actions, the power lies,

To shape a world where everyone
thrives.

How wonderful it is, this truth we hold
dear,

That with every choice, every step we
steer,

We can improve the world, make it
shine,

In this journey together, let's
intertwine.

Chandan Malana

Quote 31

"Our lives are a tapestry, woven with each moment, Each thread an opportunity to make life potent, With every chance, lies the power to improve, Embrace the moment, let your compassion groove."

Chandan Malana

Need Is Great, The Possibilities Endless

The need is great, it calls to us,

To rise above and make a fuss,

In every corner, every land,

A helping heart, a helping hand.

The opportunities abound,

To spread compassion all around,

To heal the wounds, to ease the pain,

To bring hope where it's almost slain.

Let's bridge the gap, let's lend a hand,

In every way that we can stand,

For every act, big or small,

Can make a difference, one and all.

In laughter shared, in tears we mend,

In kindness shown, we can transcend,

The troubles that this world may bear,

And show others that we truly care.

No task too small, no dream too grand,

Together, we can take a stand,

To feed the hungry, shelter the weak,

To uplift souls that feel so bleak.

With open hearts and open minds,

We'll leave no one in need behind,

For love and empathy will guide,

As we strive to make the world wide.

In every corner, every place,

The need is there, we can embrace,

The power within us, so strong,

To make a difference all lifelong.

So let us join, hand in hand,

To spread compassion through the
land,

For in each act, we have the chance,

To make a difference, and enhance.

Chandan Malana

Quote 32

"The need may be great, but with each day, Opportunities to make a difference come our way. With hearts open and a willingness to lend a hand, We can inspire change and make a stand."

Chandan Malana

Noble Deeds, Fruits Or Seeds?

In deeds we find the essence of our
might,

For actions shape the path we tread
with might,

It's not the fruit alone, but what we do,

That truly marks the difference we
pursue.

To choose the right when shadows
cloud our way,

Requires a strength that lingers day by
day,

For though we yearn to see the fruits
unfold,

It's in the present moment we are bold.

The power may elude us in this hour,

Yet still we strive to wield a greater
power,

For time is but a tapestry we weave,

And in our actions, destinies conceive.

Doubt not the worth of every noble act,

Though clouds may veil the truth, hold firm, intact,

For in the seeds of virtue, dormant, lie,

The potential to uplift and edify.

The harvest may not come within our span,

But still we sow, with resolute command,

For life's sweet yield is not for us to know,

Yet onward we press, our purpose in tow.

For in the realm of action, seeds are
sown,

A legacy that echoes on, unknown,

And though we may not see the
blossoms bloom,

The seeds we plant may yield in
distant gloom.

So let us strive, regardless of the gain,

To do what's right, and banish
thoughts of vain,

For in our hearts, the noblest virtues
stir,

And in our deeds, the power to confer.

Remember, in the face of doubt and
fear,

That actions, not outcomes, make the
sphere,

Embrace the journey, leave no task
undone,

For in our actions, a difference is won.

Chandan Malana

Quote 33

"Right action triumphs, fruit or not, A noble deed, a worthy plot, Do what's right, in every chance, Fruitful results, or just a glance."

Chandan Malana

One Chance For Change

In this fleeting life we live,

A single chance, we must believe.

To make a difference, big or small,

And leave a mark before we fall.

For you do only live once, they say,

So let us seize each precious day.

With heart ablaze and purpose strong,

We'll strive to right the world's wrong.

If I can touch a soul in need,

Plant a seed of hope, indeed,

Then I've fulfilled my destined role,

To bring forth change and make hearts
whole.

For in this vast and wondrous place,

A single act can leave a trace,

And if my actions light the way,

I'll have made a difference, come what
may.

Let kindness be my guiding light,

To banish darkness with its might.

For in a world that often grieves,

Compassion's touch can grant reprieve.

I'll lend a hand to those in pain,

Embrace their hearts through wind
and rain.

For if I ease one troubled mind,

I've made a difference of a kind.

So let us pledge, with spirits bright,

To make a difference, day and night.

For in this fleeting life we find,

Our chance to leave our mark behind.

If we can bring a smile or cheer,

Erase a pain, calm every fear,

Then we have lived as we should be,

Making a difference, setting hearts free.

Chandan Malana

Quote 34

"One chance is all we've got to make a mark, On this planet that's both wondrous and stark, If we strive to leave it better than we found, Our time on earth will have been truly profound."

Chandan Malana

One Person's Might: A World's Bright

In a world so vast, where dreams collide,

One person can make a difference, turn the tide.

No need for grandeur or wealth untold,

It's the belief in oneself, a story to unfold.

You don't have to be a big shot, a star
so bright,

For change starts within, in the
darkest night.

With courage as your compass, and
passion as your guide,

You'll navigate the currents, where
hope will reside.

Influence may elude, yet faith shall
prevail,

As the smallest voice can whisper,
break through the veil.

Each word, each action, a ripple in
time,

Creating waves of transformation,
sublime.

The power to change things lies deep in
your heart,

Embrace it with love, let it set you
apart.

For every act of kindness, no matter
how small,

Can touch a soul, inspire, and enthrall.

Plant seeds of compassion, let empathy
grow,

Nurture understanding, let tolerance
show.

For unity and harmony, they start
within,

A single person's choice, where new
beginnings begin.

The world yearns for heroes, who stand
against strife,

But true heroes emerge from the
essence of life.

They're ordinary people, with
extraordinary dreams,

Who ignites the spark of change,
through the simplest means.

So have faith in your power, let it
shine bright,

Illuminate the path, banish shadows
from sight.

For one person can make a difference,
it's true,

Believe in your potential, let your
spirit breakthrough.

*In this grand tapestry, we all play a
part,*

*With love as our armor, we'll heal
every heart.*

*Together we'll create a world that's
sublime,*

*Where one person's difference echoes
for all time.*

Chandan Malana

Quote 35

"Whether you're small or great in size, Your actions can make a difference in others' eyes, Don't underestimate the power you ways possess, Believe in yourself, and create a path to success."

Chandan Malana

Power Of Hands: We Can Change Lands

We hold the power within our grasp,

To shape a future that's free at last.

Together we stand, with hearts ablaze,

To change the world in countless ways.

Let kindness flow from our gentle
touch,

Illuminate dark corners, oh, so much.

With empathy's flame, let's bridge the
divide,

In unity, our strength will surely
reside.

Each step we take, a ripple in time,

Our actions profound, like a poet's
rhyme.

In every smile shared, a beacon of light,

Dispelling the shadows, bringing hope
to sight.

Through compassion's lens, we shall
perceive,

The struggles of others, and their
hearts relieve.

For a single act of love, so pure,

Can ignite a spark that will endure.

With open hearts, let's sow the seeds,

Of harmony and unity, fulfilling needs.

By standing tall, we can surely impart,

A legacy of change, felt in every heart.

Let's lend a hand to the weak and meek,

Embrace the outcasts, the lonely and
bleak.

With courage as our guide, we'll walk
the way,

Creating a better world, day by day.

No challenge too great, no mountain
too high,

As we strive together, we'll touch the
sky.

With determination as our guiding
force,

We'll shape a future, where all can
rejoice.

So let's embrace the power we possess,

To transform the world, and bring
forth success.

In our hands lies the strength to
rearrange,

And make a difference that will forever
change.

Chandan Malana

Quote 36

"We hold the key to a brighter earth, To thrive with love, a world of worth, With hands held high, and hearts so true, Together we'll make a change that's new."

Chandan Malana

Power Of Small Deeds

Do your little bit of good each day,

In the world where you stand, make a way.

With kindness and compassion, let it shine,

For it's in those little acts, we intertwine.

A smile offered to a stranger passing
by,

Can lighten their burden, lift them up
high.

Small gestures of love, like seeds sown,

Can grow into a garden where hope is
known.

Extend a helping hand to those in need,

For it's in unity, we truly succeed.

A word of encouragement, so gentle
and kind,

Can mend a broken spirit, heal a
wounded mind.

Speak up for justice, against what's
wrong,

In the face of adversity, stay strong.

Each voice matters, in the chorus we
sing,

Together, we can make the bells of
change ring.

Support a cause, lend a listening ear,

For empathy's power can dispel all
fear.

The little bits of good, when shared in
unity,

Create a ripple effect of love's
continuity.

Give of your time, your talents, your
heart,

In every moment, let kindness be the
art.

For in the tapestry of life, we're all
connected,

Our collective actions, a legacy
reflected.

Believe in the power of your small
deeds,

In making a difference, fulfilling noble
needs.

Embrace the truth that greatness can
be found,

In the little bits of good, beautifully
profound.

So, do your little bit of good, wherever
you stand,

For it's those little bits that make the
grand.

With love as your guide, let your light
unfurl,

And watch as the world transforms
with each little pearl.

Chandan Malana

Quote 37

"Be the light in the dark, shine where you stand, Each small act of kindness can change life's demands, A little bit of good, a selfless deed, Can inspire others to follow and succeed."

Chandan Malana

Rent We All Pay, Each And Every Day

Service to others, a rent to be paid,

In this earthly dwelling where we all
have stayed.

For the room we're granted, a purpose
we find,

To make a difference, leaving no soul
behind.

With open hearts, let's lend a helping
hand,

Extend compassion across the land.

Through selfless acts, our spirits take
flight,

Illuminating darkness with love's pure
light.

Each person's journey, unique and
diverse,

Yet united we stand, in service we
immerse.

From simple gestures to grand
endeavors,

Together we strive to make lives better,
forever.

In the smiles we share and the tears we
wipe,

In the words we speak and the wounds
we stripe,

The rent we pay is not measured in
gold,

But in the kindness and empathy we
unfold.

No room for indifference, no room for
greed,

For service to others is the noblest
creed.

We sow seeds of hope, where despair
once grew,

Making a difference in all that we do.

From comforting the lonely to feeding
the poor,

From educating minds to healing
hearts sore,

In service we discover our purpose and
worth,

Leaving footprints of love upon this
earth.

So let us rise, with passion and grace,

Embracing the opportunity to embrace,

The chance to uplift, to make burdens
light,

To serve one another, day and night.

For service to others is the rent we all
pay,

A debt we honor, each and every day.

In making a difference, our souls find
rebirth,

Service to others, the greatest legacy
on earth.

Chandan Malana

Quote 38

"To leave a mark on the world, to make our purpose known, We must give to others, for in generosity lies our own growth, For the debts we owe in every breath given, we must disown, And pay our rent with service, to humanity's utmost worth."

Chandan Malana

Road To Peace

Peace is the solace, not a fanciful
dream,

A journey of labor, where compromises
gleam.

Through battles of strife and struggles
untold,

Tiny victories won, their stories
unfold.

It's not a mirage, but a path to pursue,

Where harmony blossoms, in shades of
all hue.

With every step taken, a difference we
make,

Amidst chaos and noise, a tranquil
break.

Peace isn't bestowed on a silver platter,

But crafted with patience, and words
that matter.

In the realm of discord, where conflicts
arise,

Peace emerges gently, to our own
surprise.

It's not an illusion, a fleeting illusion,

But a tapestry woven with deep
resolution.

Through negotiations tough, we mend
the divide,

Peace takes root steadily, as egos
subside.

It's not a fantasy, an unattainable
quest,

But a relentless effort to bring out our
best.

With empathy and love, we bridge the
divide,

Peace emerges stronger, as hearts
coincide.

In the midst of chaos, it may seem
absurd,

But peace is a whisper that should be
heard.

Through brutal compromises, we find
our way,

To transform darkness into a brighter
day.

Peace doesn't come easy, it's not a
quick fix,

But through determination, we break
the matrix.

With each act of kindness, we make a
dent,

In the armor of hatred, bringing
contentment.

So let us strive together, hand in hand,

To create a world where peace will
expand.

For peace is the opposite of dreaming
alone,

It's a journey we embark on, not on our
own.

Chandan Malana

Quote 39

"*Dreams may give us hope and wings to soar, But peace is a reality that isn't easy to ignore, Tiny victories and brutal compromises we need, As we sow the seeds of peace with love and heed.*"

Chandan Malana

Service To All, A Joyful Call

In life's grand tapestry, a truth is revealed,

That joy is found when selflessness is sealed.

When hearts embrace a purpose beyond their own,

And seek to make a difference, seeds of love are sown.

To look upon our lives as humble
stewards we must,

For joy's true essence lies in serving
others' trust.

A mission defined, a noble cause to
embrace,

To spread compassion and kindness,
leaving a trace.

No longer shall happiness be a solitary
goal,

But a shared experience that heals the
soul.

In reaching out to those who are in
need,

We find our purpose, our spirits freed.

For joy can only thrive when self is set
aside,

And empathy becomes our
compassionate guide.

To uplift the weary, bring smiles to the
forlorn,

To offer hope and solace, a world
reborn.

In every act of service, a purpose comes
alive,

A chance to touch lives, to help others
thrive.

For joy's sweet melody, a symphony
profound,

Is found in making a difference, its
echoes resound.

No longer chained to selfish desires'
hold,

Our hearts awaken, compassion
unfolds.

For joy is real when selflessness is
embraced,

And in the lives we touch, its beauty is
traced.

Let us cast aside the veils of
self-centered strife,

And forge a path of meaning,
transforming life.

With every gesture, every kind word
we share,

Joy blossoms, diffusing love
everywhere.

So let us seek a purpose beyond our
own gain,

And in service, true fulfillment we
attain.

For joy is magnified when we make a
difference,

And find our true calling in love's
existence.

Chandan Malana

244

Quote 40

"Look beyond, serve with heart, Joy unbounded, here to impart, A life of purpose, beyond the self, A greater joy, for all to delve."

Chandan Malana

Simple Acts,
Matter Of Fact

In this vast world where we reside,

Each of us holds a power inside.

To make a difference, big or small,

A helping hand extended for all.

No grandiose acts are required,

Just a simple gesture admired.

Watch the neighbor's kid with care,

Ease her burdens, show you're there.

Befriend someone who's feeling low,

A ray of light when shadows grow.

Not a home, but a place they'll find,

A refuge warm, a peace of mind.

Food for the hungry, souls in need,

A vital deed, a worthy deed.

With open hearts, extend a hand,

For kindness spreads throughout the
land.

Each solitary day presents,

An opportunity to make sense.

Embrace the chance to lend a hand,

And help those who can't withstand.

A smile, a word, a tender touch,

Can heal the wounds that hurt so
much.

Our acts of kindness intertwine,

Creating ripples, love's design.

Through selfless acts, we find our
worth,

Transforming lives, bringing forth
mirth.

For in the end, what truly feeds,

Is knowing we've met others' needs.

So let us strive, together strong,

To right the world that's gone so
wrong.

For with each act, we redefine,

The power we possess, divine.

Chandan Malana

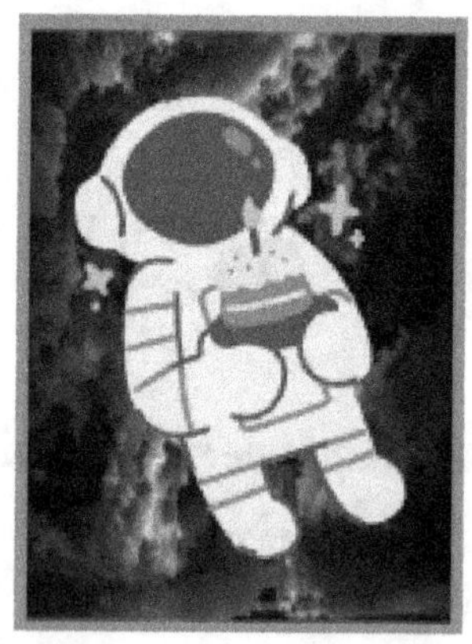

Quote 41

"Act of kindness, a simple deed,
Helping hands and in times of need,
Befriend with love, not expecting pay,
Sunshine of hope, brightening the day."

Chandan Malana

Small Acts Can Change History's Course

Few souls hold the power to shape the
course,

To bend the arcs of history with force.

Yet in each heart, a spark can ignite,

A drive to change the world, however
slight.

For in the countless acts of courage
pure,

And steadfast beliefs that endure,

Human history finds its molding
hands,

Crafted by the brave in diverse lands.

When one man rises for an ideal,

Or aids the suffering, their wounds to
heal,

Or battles the chains of injustice tight,

A ripple of hope takes flight in the
night.

From million centers, those ripples
blend,

A symphony of energy, they transcend,

They weave together, a current so
strong,

That even mightiest walls won't last
long.

So let us embrace our power and
might,

To stand for what's just, for what is
right,

Each small deed, a droplet in the
stream,

Contributing to the grander scheme.

From classrooms to homes, in streets
and in squares,

In fields of passion, where hope
repairs,

Our actions, however humble they
seem,

Can shape a future far beyond our
dream.

For in the unity of countless souls,

The waves of change surge, their power
unfolds,

With each step we take, each choice we
make,

We paint a landscape where justice
won't break.

So let us be brave, and let us believe,

That through our actions, we can achieve,

A world transformed, where love will persist,

And each small act can make a difference.

Chandan Malana

Quote 42

"*Change may seem impossible on a grand scale, But small acts of courage can never fail, It starts with one person standing tall, Sending forth ripples of hope that can heal us all.*"

Chandan Malana

Strength In Solitude, A Single Soul's Attitude

I am only one, a solitary soul,

Yet within me lies a power to make the whole,

I cannot do everything, that much is true,

But I can do something, and that's what I'll pursue.

I'll not be discouraged by limits I may
face,

For in my heart, a purpose I embrace,

Though small my impact, it can still
ignite,

A flame of change, to bring about
what's right.

In every action I take, no matter how
small,

I'll strive to make a difference, stand
tall,

For it's not the grand gestures, but the
seeds we sow,

That grows into movements, helping
others to know.

I won't let my limitations dampen my
zeal,

For within my reach, there's much I
can reveal,

A kind word, a helping hand, a
compassionate ear,

These simple acts can erase pain and
fear.

The world may seem vast, problems
overwhelming,

But I'll focus on the moments, the lives
worth transforming,

With empathy as my guide, I'll lend my
voice,

And let compassion ripple, making
hearts rejoice.

Each step I take, a ripple in the pond,

A testament to the belief I respond,

That even one person, with
determination and grace,

Can bring about change, in this chaotic
space.

So I'll march forward, undeterred by
what I lack,

Knowing my efforts, though humble,
won't backtrack,

For in unity with others, together we'll
find,

That the sum of our actions can truly
redefine.

I am only one, but I am one indeed,

With strength to plant the seed, help
those in need,

I'll focus on what's within my grasp,
my light,

And let it shine brightly, making a
difference, day and night.

Chandan Malana

Quote 43

"Though one may feel too small to make an impact, A single soul can take a step and enact, For in the power of one, lies the chance, To make a difference, to make a change, to advance."

Chandan Malana

Thought Divine, In Smallest Size To Shine

Anyone who thinks they're too petite,

To shape the world with a touch so sweet,

Has never known the power they possess,

In moments of stillness and quiet finesse.

For in the darkness, when all seems
still,

A buzzing presence can cause a thrill,

A tiny mosquito, a nuisance, it seems,

But its impact lingers, disrupting
dreams.

With each tiny bite, a reminder clear,

That even the small can instill a fear,

A single action, a ripple profound,

Can echo loudly, without making a
sound.

The buzzing persists, relentless and
low,

Provoking frustration that starts to
grow,

But in that annoyance lies a subtle
truth,

That even the humble can inspire
youth.

In the vast tapestry of this world we
share,

Every voice, every being, has a layer to
bear,

No matter how humble, how seemingly
small,

We each possess the power to stand
tall.

A mosquito's persistence, a reminder
true,

That size is no measure of what we can
do,

From the tiniest acts to the grandest of
all,

We can shape the world, no matter how
small.

So let not doubt overshadow your
might,

Embrace your potential, shine forth
your light,

For in the quiet moments, great change
can ignite,

And those who believe will always take
flight.

So remember this lesson from the
mosquito's zoom,

Anyone can make a difference, even in
a room,

No matter your size or the challenges
you face,

Believe in your power, let your impact
embrace.

Chandan Malana

Quote 44

"Size may deceive, but within lies the might, For even the smallest can shape the fight. The tiniest acts can shape the grandest change, No soul is too small, no impact too strange."

Chandan Malana

To Give Is To Live

When passion fuels your every move,
And purpose guides the path you
choose,
A life of meaning, you can't deny,
For in your hands, you make a
difference, oh so spry.

With every step, a legacy you weave,
A tapestry of love and deeds,
For when you cease to make a
contribution,
The spark within begins to fade, in
dissolution.

The world awaits your unique touch,
Your talents, gifts, they matter much,
Embrace the calling, let your light
shine,
For in your actions, a difference will
define.

Each word you speak, each gesture
kind,
Creates ripples, echoes in mankind,
Touching hearts, igniting souls,
A symphony of change, as your
purpose unfolds.

In every smile you freely share,
In every helping hand you dare,
A profound impact starts to bloom,
A testament to life's eternal room.

When days grow long and shadows
creep,
Remember, purpose lies not in
slumber's keep,
Awake your spirit, breathe life anew,
For in your contribution, vitality will
accrue.

A life lived fully, a life well spent,
Is measured not by time, but by intent,
So leave a mark, make your presence
known,
For in making a difference, your
essence will be shown.

When the final chapter draws near,
May you look back without a fear,
Knowing you've lived with all your
might,
A legacy of contributions shining
bright.
In making a difference, our souls come
alive,
For when we cease, we truly begin to
die.

Chandan Malana

Quote 45

"When our time on this earth comes to an end, And memories are the only thing we leave to fend, May our contributions inspire others, even after we die, For that's how we leave a legacy that will always thrive."

Chandan Malana

Trees Planted For Tomorrow's Scope

In a world of wonder and strife,

Lies a truth that shapes our life.

To plant trees with love and care,

Is the essence we must declare.

With every seed we gently sow,

A legacy begins to grow.

For true meaning lies not in greed,

But in nurturing every seed.

For in the shade of trees so grand,

We find purpose, we understand.

To give without seeking return,

Is how our souls truly discern.

Though we may never rest beneath,

Their branches shielding us beneath,

Our actions ripple, far and wide,

Spreading hope with every stride.

Each sapling, a beacon of light,

Guiding others through the night.

A difference made, not for ourselves,

But for generations, boundless wells.

For life's meaning lies not in gain,

But in the lives we can sustain.

To plant a tree is to embrace,

A future where love leaves its trace.

Let us tend to Earth's sacred ground,

Where harmony and growth are found.

For under trees, in selfless bliss,

We find the true meaning of this.

So let us plant with joyful hearts,

Knowing that our love imparts.

For in the shade of trees we sow,

The true meaning of life will grow.

Chandan Malana

Quote 46

"A life's true beauty lies not in gain,
But in leaving a legacy that will
remain, Planting trees that shall
flourish for all to see, Providing shelter
for generations yet to be."

Chandan Malana

Unseen Light, Only The Brave Can Bring Into Sight

In shadows cast by doubt's fierce might,

There lies a truth, a guiding light,

If only we're brave enough to see,

The brilliance that can set us free.

Amidst the storms that life may bring,

A beacon shines, a hopeful string,

If only we're brave enough to know,

The power within us, we can show.

When darkness veils our weary hearts,

A spark ignites, new paths it charts,

If only we're brave enough to dare,

To make a difference, show we care.

In every soul, a flame does burn,

A fervent wish, a lesson learned,

If only we're brave enough to find,

The strength to leave complacency
behind.

In unity, we'll find our way,

Together we can seize the day,

If only we're brave enough to fight,

For justice, love, and what is right.

When fear consumes, and hope grows
thin,

A candle's glow can still begin,

If only we're brave enough to ignite,

The fire of change, to make things
right.

So let us rise, with hearts aglow,

Embrace the light, let kindness flow,

If only we're brave enough to be,

The difference we all long to see.

For there is always light to share,

If we choose love, and truly care,

If only we're brave enough to start,

We'll change the world, and mend each heart.

Chandan Malana

Quote 47

"The shadows may rise and cast their threat, A crushing veil of darkness that's hard to forget, But if we dare to look and be brave to see, The light will shine bright and set our hearts free."

Chandan Malana

When It's Time To Fight, Speak Out And Ignite

When injustice rises, bold and clear,

A call to action, it's time to adhere.

For when we witness a world askew,

We must step forward, our voices renew.

In the face of unfairness, we won't
abide,

In unity, we stand, side by side.

Speaking out against what's unjust,

Our convictions strong, our hearts
robust.

For what is right, we'll take a stand,

No more complacency, a resolute
demand.

With courage as our guide, we'll find a
way,

To make a difference, come what may.

When darkness veils the path ahead,

We'll kindle hope, ignite a thread.

With words that resonate, like
thunder's roar,

We'll pierce through silence,
forevermore.

The time for whispers has long since
passed,

Our voices harmonize, a chorus vast.

United, we'll ripple across the tide,

For justice and fairness, we'll not hide.

Through troubled waters, we'll forge
ahead,

With empathy and compassion, our
guiding thread.

No challenge too great, no barrier too
tall,

Together we'll rise, and break down the
wall.

In this symphony of change we weave,

Each note of progress, a hope to
conceive.

With every word, with every action we
take,

A brighter world we shall surely make.

So let us embrace this call to embark,

To shake the foundations, to leave our
mark.

For in the face of wrongs, we'll rise
above,

And through good trouble, we'll make a
difference, with love.

Chandan Malana

Quote 48

*"When wrongness stares you in the
eyes, And you see justice masked with
lies, Speak out, make noise and cause
some trouble, For only then can change
become a burst bubble."*

Chandan Malana

With Your Gentle Ways

In a gentle way, with hearts aligned,

A world of change, we can define.

With words of kindness, softly spoken,

Lives transformed, love as the token.

With tender touch and actions pure,

Compassion's ripple will endure.

In every step, a path we pave,

To make a difference, souls to save.

With open minds and listening ears,

We heal the wounds, dismiss the fears.

Embracing differences, we find,

Unity's power, love that binds.

Through humble acts, no grand
display,

We touch the lives that come our way.

A helping hand, a caring smile,

Can mend a heart, bridge the divide.

In quiet moments, subtle grace,

We find the strength to change our
space.

A single candle, in darkness gleams,

Illuminating hopes and dreams.

For in each heart, a spark resides,

A force within that love provides.

With gentle waves, we sow the seeds,

Of empathy's growth and noble deeds.

So let us strive to be the light,

To champion justice, truth, and right.

In every choice, a chance to be,

The difference that the world can see.

In a gentle way, we have the power,

To shape a world, hour by hour.

With love as guide, our actions unfurled,

In a gentle way, we'll shake the world.

Chandan Malana

Quote 49

"When gentle actions meet a kind embrace, The world around us can transform in grace, For shaking it up may be a subtle art, But the ripples of change will impact every heart."

Chandan Malana

Your Voice, Your Power, Time To Empower

Do it, oh soul, what's there to delay?

Embrace the fire that ignites your way.

Stand tall, with courage, let your heart shine.

Unleash your words, let them intertwine.

The world awaits, hungry for your
voice,

A beacon of truth, it's your righteous
choice.

Rise above doubt, let your spirit soar,

For in your conviction, change lies in
store.

No matter your station, no matter
your name,

You possess power, let it burst into
flame.

Speak for the silenced, speak for the
weak,

In your voice, the voiceless find the
strength they seek.

Don't wait for permission, don't
hesitate,

Make a difference, it's never too late.

For in your beliefs, lies a force
untamed,

Ready to kindle the world, forever
unchained.

When darkness looms and shadows
descend,

Your voice can shine bright, helping
hearts mend.

Through rhymes and rhythms, let your
message unfold,

Inspiring souls, with stories yet untold.

The tapestry of life, diverse and vast,

Your perspective matters, it will
always last.

Be the catalyst, the winds of change,

Through your words, a new era will
arrange.

Take a stand, let your passion arise,

In unity and love, the world
harmonize.

For every voice matters, no matter the
hue,

Together, let's build a world that's
anew.

So, do it, my friend, let your voice
resound,

In words and actions, let your purpose
be found.

For within you lies the power to
convey,

A message that echoes beyond today.

Chandan Malana

Quote 50

"Take the chance, don't wait too long, Stand for what's right, be brave and strong, Your voice is unique, don't hold it down, Speak up, speak out, let your beliefs be found."

Chandan Malana

Buy Me A Cup
Of Coffee

Dear readers,

Thank you so much for taking the time to read my words. If I have in some way managed to touch your life, then I am truly honoured.

I hope that my poetry and words have been able to time travel you back to any emotion and in some way, some where, somehow, in some place, in some moment touched your life then my life has become purposeful for others.

If you have enjoyed my work and would like to show your appreciation, I would be delighted if you could buy me a cup of coffee. Your support would mean the world to me. Every bit helps and I am truly grateful for your generosity. Thank you once again,

Your faithful writer

Chandan Malana

Paytm, Google pay, Phonepe, UPI

chandan.malana@paytm

****

paypal.me/ChandanMalana

****

chandanmalana@gmail.com

******

instagram.com/chandan_malana

******

EUR account details

Account holder: Chandan Malana
SWIFT/BIC: TRWIBEB1XXX
IBAN: BE75 9674 9601 8051
Wise's address:
Avenue Louise 54, Room S52
Brussels
1050
Belgium

******

GBP account details

GBP Outside the UK

Account holder: Chandan Malana
SWIFT/BIC: TRWIGB2L
IBAN: GB71 TRWI 2314 7012 4893 22
Wise's address:
56 Shoreditch High Street
London
E1 6JJ
United Kingdom

******

GBP Inside the UK

Account holder: Chandan Malana
Sort code: 23-14-70
Account number: 12489322
**IBAN: GB71 TRWI 2314 7012 4893
22**
Wise's address:
56 Shoreditch High Street
London
E1 6JJ
United Kingdom

****

USD account details

Account holder: Chandan Malana
ACH and Wire routing number:
084009519
Account number:
9600010468802671
Account type: Checking
Wise's address:
30 W. 26th Street, Sixth Floor
New York NY 10010
United States

******

BSC
BNB Smart Chain
[BEP20]

0x652347bc8ccbe876a1cd93534a1
8c6d4b7bd4d8f

Books By This Author

An Innocent Kiss

50 River Beneath 50 Ocean

Blow A Kiss

Vol. 2